1

BELLY OF THE BEAST

The Kenny Scott Story

Written by Kenneth Scott

Dedication

To my mother, for her unwavering love and strength, and to my wife Jessica, for your unconditional love, resilience, and for believing in me even when I struggled to believe in myself.

To my children—thank you for being my inspiration, my motivation, and the living proof that change is possible.

And most of all, to God—for your grace, mercy, and redemption. Without You, none of this would be possible.

The Belly Of The Beast

AUTHOR'S NOTE

This book isn't just a story—it's my truth. Every chapter, every scar, every prayer and every piece of pain you'll read is real. I didn't write this to be famous. I wrote it so the next person who feels forgotten, broken, or boxed in by the system knows they're not alone.

I was just a teenager when my life was taken off course. The streets raised me, the system tried to erase me, and for a while, I didn't know if I'd ever find my way back. But God had other plans.

Through it all—prison, betrayal, heartbreak, growth, redemption—I found something bigger than survival. I found purpose.

If you're reading this and you've been through hell, if you've sat behind bars or felt trapped in your own mind, know this: there's still a way out. Not just from the outside—but from within.

This book is for the misunderstood, the misjudged, the underestimated. It's for the ones who know what it's like to fight silent battles and keep walking anyway.

Thank you for picking up my story. I pray it inspires you to keep moving, keep believing, and never stop reaching for the light—even in the darkest places.

— Kenny Scott

Table of Contents

Introduction

They say the system is broken—but I learned early that for kids like me, especially young Black boys from places like Camden, New Jersey, the system was never designed to protect us in the first place. It was built to watch us, label us, trap us, and then throw away the key. I was just seventeen when my life changed forever—set up, lied on, betrayed, and sentenced by people who never cared about who I was or what I could've been. In a moment, I went from a young man trying to find his way… to a number in a cell.

This book isn't just a story about injustice. It's not just about one bad night, one false accusation, or even the years I lost behind bars. It's a story about pain, identity, faith, and redemption. It's about what happens when a system swallows you whole but God refuses to let your soul get buried.

I didn't come from riches or stability. I came from Camden—a city with a reputation, where you had to be tough to survive. I saw struggle every day. My mother worked herself to the bone to keep us fed, while my father battled demons of addiction during the crack era. We didn't have much, but we had each other. Still, the streets called to me. Not because I wanted to be a criminal, but because I wanted a way out. A way to provide. A way to matter.

Football was my dream. Music was my therapy. But survival? That was the priority.

Then everything changed. One ride home. One decision. One lie. That's all it took for my life to be stolen. They didn't want to hear my side. The truth didn't matter in that courtroom. The color of my skin, my address, and the badge of my accuser spoke louder than my voice ever could. I was found guilty in their minds before I ever had a chance to speak.

Inside, I faced demons I never knew existed. Anger. Depression. Hopelessness. I watched people break around me—and I came close to breaking myself. But something inside me held on. Even when I didn't want to live. Even when I questioned everything, including God.

Especially God.

But somehow, in that cold, lonely place, God met me. Not in the churchy way people talk about on Sundays. He met me in my brokenness. In my tears. In my confusion. In the silence of the night when all I had was memories and regret. He reminded me I still had purpose. That my pain wasn't the end of my story.

I started changing. Slowly. Painfully. But the shift came. I learned to forgive—not just others, but myself. I began to hope again. To believe that I could still become something. That I could still make a difference. That I could still be a father, a husband, a man of purpose.

Today, I stand not as a victim, but as a survivor. A warrior. A man of faith. I've spoken to the youth who walk the same streets I once did. I've trained others not just in fitness but in mindset. I found love, built a family, and created a life rooted in something real. That's the power of God. That's the power of healing. That's the power of truth.

I didn't write this book for sympathy. I wrote it for

the ones still in the storm. For the young brother with dreams caught up in the wrong crowd. For the mother praying her son makes it home. For the man in a cell who thinks he's forgotten. For the system to understand we are not disposable.

I wrote this book because I'm still here. And that means I've got a responsibility.

This is more than just my story. This is a call to action. A cry for justice. A message of hope. It's proof that even when the world tries to bury you, God can still resurrect you. That even from the belly of the beast, you can rise.

So before you turn the page, I ask you—read with an open heart. Hear me. See me. And if you've been through hell too, know that you're not alone. Redemption is real. Freedom is possible. And your story isn't over.

This is mine.

Welcome to The Belly of the Beast.

— Kenneth Scott

CHAPTER 1: THE HACK RIDE THAT CHANGED EVERYTHING

As a teenager growing up in Camden, New Jersey, life was always a balancing act between dreams and survival. I was passionate about football, determined to make something of myself through sports, but I was also pulled in by the street life. All my friends were in it, and it seemed like the only way to make fast cash when your parents were barely making ends meet. My mom worked two jobs just to keep food on the table. My dad, although he had a job, was struggling with addiction—a silent war that affected our whole household.

Music was my escape. R&B and hip-hop were the soundtrack to my youth, helping me make sense of the chaos around me. I was a student at Woodrow Wilson High School, playing football and trying to stay focused, but the streets always had a way of pulling you back in. That's the thing about Camden—

opportunity was scarce, but temptation was always right around the corner.

One night, everything changed. Me and my girlfriend got into a heated argument over something stupid. It wasn't even that serious, but in the moment, it felt like the world was closing in. I stormed out of the apartment without looking back, frustrated and needing space to breathe. That decision, made in anger, set off a chain of events that would alter the course of my life.

Back in the '90s, Camden had this thing called a "hack." It was like an unofficial cab service—just regular people giving rides for a few bucks. It was cheaper than a taxi and way more common. I waved one down that night, a guy I'd seen around before. He agreed to take me from downtown Camden to Cramer Hill for five dollars. As we drove, I asked if I could use his car for a little while. I offered him forty dollars to let me drive it for an hour. He agreed, no problem. That was normal back then—if you had some cash and you knew the driver, they'd let you ride out as long as you brought the car back on time.

But when I came back around to return the car, he was gone. Just vanished. I didn't think too much of it at first. Maybe he stepped away for a minute or ran an errand. Little did I know, he had gone to the police and told them I carjacked him at gunpoint at a red light. That was a flat-out lie, but the damage was already done.

I didn't know the cops were following me. I was just riding around, trying to find the hack to return his car. When I noticed the police trailing me, I panicked. I didn't understand why they were after me, but instinct kicked in. I pressed the gas and took off, trying to get away. My heart was racing. I didn't even have a weapon on me. I didn't even know I was a wanted man.

I ended up crashing the car. The whole thing spiraled out of control from there. I was arrested on the spot, confused, angry, and scared. I kept thinking it had to be some kind of mistake. But when I got to the police station, reality hit hard. The hack was there, calmly telling the police that I robbed him at gunpoint. I was in disbelief. He looked me in the face and lied without even flinching. I kept saying over and over, "This can't be real."

Later, he even admitted to wanting to drop the charges. Said he made a mistake. But by then, the system had already swallowed me up. The machine was in motion, and nothing I said could stop it. I was seventeen years old, and in one night, my entire future was stolen. My dreams of college ball, of making it out, of doing right by my family—gone. Just like that.

At that moment, I lost my faith in the justice system. I lost my faith in people. I even started losing my faith in God. But this was only the beginning. I was about to be thrown into a world where innocence didn't matter, where survival meant becoming something you never thought you'd be.

This was the night I entered the belly of the beast.

The Belly Of The Beast

Reflection Questions – Chapter 1: *The Hack Ride That Changed Everything*

1. Have you ever made a quick decision out of emotion that changed your life? What might you have done differently in hindsight?

2. How does your environment shape the choices you make, especially as a young person?

3. Do you believe the justice system is fair to everyone? Why or why not?

4. How would you react if someone falsely accused you of something serious? What support would you need in that moment?

5. What role has faith (or the loss of it) played during difficult times in your life?

The Belly Of The Beast

CHAPTER 2: BABY TRENTON

After the arrest, everything moved like a blur. I was still seventeen—just a kid—but the system didn't treat me like one. It didn't see my fear, my confusion, or my cries for help. All it saw was a case to process. I wasn't Kenneth Scott anymore; I was just another number in the machine.

They sent me to a juvenile facility known as Baby Trenton, officially called the Juvenile Medium Security Facility in Bordentown, New Jersey. But everyone called it Baby Trenton. It didn't take long for me to realize this place was designed to break boys like me. It was dark, cold, and full of kids who had been failed by life just like I had. Some were angry, some were numb, but all of us were trapped— physically and mentally.

At first, I tried to keep to myself. I was still in shock from everything that had happened. But you can't be quiet too long in a place like that. Silence gets tested.

Weakness gets hunted. I learned quickly that if I wanted to survive, I couldn't be the same kid I was on the outside. I had to become what they wanted me to be: hard, unfeeling, dangerous. That place turned boys into monsters.

I saw fights nearly every day. There were kids getting jumped in the bathrooms, guards turning a blind eye, and some even encouraging the violence. You learned fast who to avoid and when to keep your head down. I remember lying awake at night in my cell, listening to the sounds of yelling, banging, and sometimes, crying. Nobody talked about it in the morning, but we all heard it.

My attitude started to shift. I stopped caring. I stopped hoping. I thought, maybe this is who I am now. Maybe there's no way back. But even in that darkness, God wasn't done with me yet.

That's when I met Isam.

Isam was one of the older guys in there, but different. He wasn't loud or wild like the rest. He carried himself with calm and strength. We started talking, and for the first time, I felt like someone saw me—not the charges, not the anger, but me. He told me that God still had a plan for my life, even if I couldn't see it. At first, I brushed him off. I was angry with God. I felt abandoned. But he kept showing up, kept checking on me. Kept praying for me even when I couldn't pray for myself.

Little by little, something changed. I started listening. I started reading scripture again. I started believing— maybe not all the way, but enough to shift my mindset. Isam kept me grounded 100%. He reminded me that no matter what the system tried to turn me into, I still had a choice. I didn't have to give in.

I stopped fighting. I stopped getting into trouble. I started thinking about my family, about getting out, about who I wanted to be. Baby Trenton didn't let up, but I did. I let go of the anger, the pride, and started to focus on growth. That shift didn't just save me—it planted a seed that would grow later in ways I couldn't yet imagine.

The Belly Of The Beast

Reflection Questions – Chapter 2: *Baby Trenton*

6. How does your environment impact the person you become?

7. Have you ever had to adapt or change yourself in order to survive? Was that change temporary or lasting?

8. Who has shown up in your life during a dark time and helped you see a different path?

9. What does it mean to stay grounded in a place designed to break you?

10.   What role can faith or mentorship play in healing from trauma?

The Belly Of The Beast

CHAPTER 3: SHIFTING FAITH

By the time I left Baby Trenton, I was no longer the same boy who walked in. Something inside me had hardened, but something else had also awakened. I carried a quiet determination to survive and make it out, not just physically but mentally and spiritually. Still, I had a long road ahead of me.

They transferred me to a harsher facility as I got older. This wasn't juvenile anymore—this was where young men were molded by violence, fear, and the cold reality of time. It was a different world, where you had to watch your back at every corner. Respect was currency, and weakness could cost you everything.

The early days were filled with tension. I had learned enough at Baby Trenton to know when to speak and when to stay silent, but the rules here were different. The politics ran deeper. I watched how the older guys moved, how alliances were formed, how silence wasn't just safety—it was strategy. I kept my head down, listened, and adapted.

But inside, I was battling something more complex. I wasn't just angry anymore—I was questioning everything. Why did God let this happen? Why me? Was there really a purpose in all of this pain? There were nights I stared at the ceiling of my cell and cried silently, not just out of sadness but confusion. I had started believing again at Baby Trenton, but now I wasn't so sure. It felt like God had hit pause. Like He forgot.

One day, I heard a sermon playing on a radio down the hall. I don't know who was playing it or why, but something about the preacher's voice cut through the noise in my soul. He said, "Sometimes, the pit is the process. You can't get to purpose without passing through pain."

That stuck with me. I wrote it down on a scrap of paper and kept it in my Bible. Even when I doubted, I held onto that line. Maybe, just maybe, there was still something greater waiting for me on the other side of this nightmare.

Over time, I started opening back up to God. Not in a loud or showy way—just in quiet prayers, little reflections, small moments of trust. I started journaling again, reading scriptures slowly, letting the words work on my heart. And I began to feel something shift. Not overnight, but gradually. The bitterness began to dull. My heart began to soften.

There was still anger. Still pain. Still injustice. But now, there was also hope. A fragile, flickering hope that maybe my story wasn't over. That maybe this prison wasn't the end, but the middle.

And for the first time in a long time, I started to believe that healing was possible.

Reflection Questions – Chapter 3:
Shifting Faith

11.   Have you ever questioned your faith during a difficult time? What brought you back—or what kept you distant?

12.   What role does pain play in personal growth or spiritual development?

13.   Can you remember a moment when a small sign or message helped you hold on?

14.   How do you find purpose in situations that feel hopeless or unfair?

15.   What does healing mean to you, and how do you know when it begins?

CHAPTER 4: FINDING PEACE IN THE CHAOS

Prison was loud—even when it was quiet. The clank of doors, the echo of voices, the tension in the air—it never truly stopped. But somehow, in the middle of all that noise, I started to find something I never expected: peace.

It didn't come all at once. At first, it was just a few moments here and there—times when I'd wake up early, before the unit got noisy, and read my Bible in the dim light. Or when I'd sit at the edge of my bunk and journal what I was feeling instead of lashing out. Small things. But those moments started to add up. I began to realize that peace wasn't something given to me—I had to choose it, over and over again, even in the middle of chaos.

I started watching the other guys. Some of them were trapped in a cycle—fighting, gambling, getting into trouble just to feel alive. But others? They were building. Reading. Writing. Working out. Trying to stay sane. I saw the difference, and I knew which path I wanted to be on. I was tired of the anger. Tired of waking up each day with nothing but pain and resentment. I had to find another way.

Working out became a major part of my routine. It started as a way to release frustration, but it turned into a discipline. Pushups, sit-ups, burpees, makeshift weights—whatever I could do to push my body and clear my mind. There was something powerful about feeling sore after a hard workout, something that reminded me I was still alive, still in control of something. The more I focused on fitness, the more grounded I felt. It gave me structure in a place built on chaos.

Even my cell became a space of transformation. I made my bed every morning, even though no one cared. I kept my belongings neat. I lit a mental candle in the dark, telling myself: "If you can control your space, you can start to control your mind." And slowly, that became true.

I also started helping other guys who wanted to change. A couple of younger dudes came to me asking for advice on how to deal with their time. I didn't have all the answers, but I told them what worked for me. Before long, we were holding each other accountable—reading together, working out together, praying together. We formed a small circle of sanity in a place designed to drive people mad.

There was one young dude—Marcus—barely eighteen. He reminded me a lot of myself. Lost. Angry. Distrusting. But over time, I watched him open up, start to write poems, start to hope again. I'll never forget the day he said, "Yo, Kenny, you make this place feel less like hell." That broke me in a good way. That let me know what I was doing mattered.

It wasn't easy. There were days I slipped, days when anger still got the best of me. Sometimes a guard would say something slick and my blood would boil. Sometimes I'd hear bad news from home and feel that old rage rise back up. But even then, I bounced back quicker. I started recognizing the warning signs in myself and learning how to respond instead of react. That was new for me.

I began thinking more about the future. I wanted to do something with my life—not just survive, but serve. I started writing down ideas for when I got out. Maybe I could mentor kids. Maybe I could help prevent someone else from going through what I went through. I wrote a whole list one night: "Open a gym. Start a nonprofit. Write my story. Be a better man."

That vision—faint at first—became my anchor. It gave my time meaning. It gave my pain a purpose. I realized that I had something valuable: my story, my testimony, my scars. I could use them.

And through that, I found peace—not in my surroundings, but within myself.

Reflection Questions – Chapter 4: *Finding Peace in the Chaos*

16. Have you ever found peace in a chaotic or painful situation? What helped you get there?

17. What routines or practices help keep you grounded during hard times?

18. How do you decide who or what to align yourself with in difficult environments?

19. Can discipline be a form of healing? Why or why not?

20. What role does service—helping others—play in your own growth and recovery?

CHAPTER 5: BROTHERS, BARS, AND BREAKTHROUGHS

Prison had a way of making time feel like it was both standing still and slipping through your fingers. Some days felt endless—just the same walls, same faces, same routines. But other times, moments hit you that changed everything. Moments when someone said something, or you saw something, and suddenly the whole place looked different. Chapter 5 of my story was filled with those moments.

One of the biggest turning points came when I was transferred again, this time to a new unit with a mix of guys from all over the state. It was rough at first— new faces, new tensions, new politics. You had to figure out fast who was real and who was dangerous. But that's also where I met Rob and Darius—two guys who would become like brothers to me.

Rob was from Newark—loud, smart, always joking but never sloppy. He had been down for a few years already and had a reputation for staying out of the drama. Darius was quieter, more thoughtful, a reader and deep thinker. He carried books everywhere. We started talking in the yard one day about working out, then about music, then life. That was the spark.

We formed a tight bond. Not a gang, not a clique— just three brothers trying to stay focused in the middle of madness. We worked out together, prayed together, and pushed each other to stay sharp. We made promises that we were going to make it out and do better. We talked about plans—businesses, family, healing. We even created a notebook full of dreams. Rob wanted to start a trucking company. Darius wanted to open a bookstore and teach kids how to write. Me? I wanted to turn my pain into power. I told them I was going to start something for the youth—a fitness center that was more than just weights. A place where boys could become men, the right way.

That bond kept me sane. It reminded me that even in the darkest places, you could still find light in people.

Rob would crack jokes that made you forget where you were, even just for a second. Darius would share quotes from books that made you think deeper about your own life. We challenged each other—mentally, spiritually, physically. There were mornings we'd run laps in the yard while the others were still asleep, pushing ourselves to stay ready, stay sharp. That kind of discipline created strength that no bars could take away.

But not everyone wanted to see us focused. Some guys mocked us. Some guards tried to provoke us. That was the real test—not just staying out of trouble, but staying committed to a future we couldn't even see yet. Sometimes it felt like walking through fire, knowing you could get burned, but walking anyway.

One night, there was a fight in the unit. A big one. Alarms went off, people got hurt, and I had a choice to make. I had been close to getting pulled in, but I stepped back. I walked away. That moment shook me. Not just because I avoided trouble, but because I realized I was different now. The old me would've been in the middle of it. But now, I had something to lose: my future.

Later that night, I sat in my cell and stared at the ceiling for hours. I thought about my mom. I thought about all the nights she cried, trying to hold the family together while I was locked away. I thought about my siblings, my community, my younger self. I couldn't go back, but I could move forward. And that night, I picked up a pen.

I wrote a letter to myself. I called it a "breakthrough letter." I wrote everything I had been through—the pain, the anger, the small victories. I told myself I was proud. That I wasn't a victim anymore. That I had survived the belly of the beast, and I was still standing.

I wrote until my hand hurt. I cried while I wrote. But when I was done, I felt lighter. I folded that letter and tucked it inside my Bible. It was a reminder that no matter how deep the pit, I was climbing out. That I was no longer just a number—I was a man becoming.

And for the first time in a long time, I believed it.

Reflection Questions – Chapter 5: *Brothers, Bars, and Breakthroughs*

21.   Who are the people in your life who keep you grounded and focused?

22.   How do you handle being in a space where not everyone wants to see you grow?

23.   What does brotherhood or sisterhood mean to you, especially in difficult times?

24.   Have you ever had a moment where you recognized growth in yourself? What triggered it?

25.   What dreams have you written down that still guide you today?

CHAPTER 6: PREPARING FOR RELEASE

As the years passed, the idea of release went from a distant fantasy to a looming reality. It was surreal. I had been down so long, I almost forgot what freedom felt like. But now it was coming. And while most people might think that's a reason to celebrate, for me, it brought a mix of excitement, fear, and uncertainty.

Getting out sounds simple—just walk out the gates and never look back. But anyone who's been incarcerated knows it's more complicated than that. You don't just reenter the world like you never left. Time moves on without you. People change. Places change. And if you haven't changed too, you're bound to fall right back into the same traps.

I started thinking seriously about who I wanted to be on the outside. I wasn't that same seventeen-year-old kid anymore. I had been tested, broken, rebuilt. And I wasn't going to waste my second chance. I made a list of goals and taped it to the wall beside my bunk: stay out of trouble, find honest work, reconnect with family, give back, stay close to God.

Preparation became my full-time job. I enrolled in every program I could—vocational training, life skills, reentry support. I took welding classes, learned how to type and build resumes, and even joined a financial literacy workshop. I didn't want to just get by—I wanted to thrive. I talked to mentors and counselors, asking real questions about how to manage stress, how to budget, how to find housing. I wrote letters to organizations and nonprofits asking for guidance. I wasn't just preparing to leave—I was preparing to live.

Some days were harder than others. There were mornings I'd wake up feeling anxious, wondering if I was truly ready. I'd replay the past in my mind— everything I'd done, everything that had happened to me. But then I'd remind myself of how far I'd come. I wasn't that scared kid anymore. I had knowledge now. I had purpose.

The emotional part was just as tough. There was fear. Fear of failing. Fear of being rejected. Fear that I might come home and feel like a stranger in my own city. Camden had changed. My family had changed. I had changed. I had a niece I had never met, old friends I didn't talk to anymore, streets that weren't the same. Part of me wondered—would Camden still have space for someone like me?

I prayed every night for strength and guidance. I asked God not just to open doors, but to prepare my heart for what was waiting on the other side. Sometimes I'd sit in silence and just imagine it—my first meal, the feel of real clothes, the sound of home. I thought about hugging my mom again, seeing my sister, breathing real air without fences around me. That vision kept me going. That hope became my fuel.

I also thought about the responsibilities waiting for me. I couldn't afford to come out and wing it. I had to have a plan. I knew I wanted to work in fitness. I wanted to get certified as a personal trainer. I even mapped out how I'd enroll in community college. I visualized myself opening a gym—not just a place to work out, but a center for mentorship, community, and growth. I wasn't just dreaming—I was preparing for it like my life depended on it.

Other guys in the unit were getting close to release too. Some of them were scared. Others were cocky, pretending like they had it all figured out. I stayed humble. I stayed focused. I knew the real battle would start once I was out. I didn't want to be another number that returned. I wanted to make it count.

Then one day, the release date became official. I stared at the paper for what felt like hours. I had dreamed about that moment for so long, and now it was real. I cried. Not just from joy, but from the weight of it all. I thought about everything I had survived—the lies, the violence, the loneliness, the silence. I had survived. And now I had to prove—to myself, to my family, to the world—that I could thrive.

I folded that release notice and tucked it in my Bible. Right next to the breakthrough letter I had written in the last unit. Those two pieces of paper reminded me of where I had been and where I was going. They reminded me that faith, focus, and growth were not just words—they were my reality.

And I promised myself, right then and there, that I would never go back—not just to prison, but to the mindset that landed me there.

Reflection Questions – Chapter 6:
Preparing for Release

26.　　What does true preparation for a major life change look like to you?

27.　　How can fear both motivate and paralyze someone during a transition?

28.　　What steps can you take to make sure change is lasting and not temporary?

29.　　What are some things you would want to do differently if given a second chance?

30.　　How do you reconnect with a world that has moved on without you?

Chapter 7 First Steps to Freedom

The morning I was released didn't feel real. I woke up before the sun, wide-eyed in a still-dark cell that had held me for years. My heart was pounding—not from fear this time, but from possibility. This was it. The day I had imagined a thousand different ways. But now that it had come, I didn't know whether to smile or cry.

The guards called my name, and I packed up everything I had: a few letters, a notebook full of reflections, and a mind full of hope. I left my Bible open to the same verse I had read every night for the past year—Jeremiah 29:11: "For I know the plans I have for you," declares the Lord. I didn't know exactly what those plans looked like, but I was ready to find out.

Walking down that corridor for the last time felt like leaving a different version of myself behind. Every step echoed memories—of pain, growth, rage, healing. I was no longer the same man who entered. I had scars, but I also had purpose.

Stepping outside the gates was like breathing for the first time. The air felt different. The sun hit my face in a way I hadn't felt in years. And then I saw my mom. She was standing there, tears in her eyes, arms wide open. I ran to her like a child. In that moment, I didn't care who was watching. That hug reminded me why I had fought so hard to change.

The ride home was quiet but powerful. Camden looked both familiar and foreign. Stores had changed. Buildings were torn down. People I knew were gone. But something in me had changed too—I wasn't just returning to the city. I was returning as a new man.

That first week was overwhelming. The world moved fast. Smartphones, apps, touchscreens—technology had leaped forward while I was frozen in time. I had to relearn everything from how to navigate the internet to how to hold a normal conversation without watching my back. I was afraid to cross the street without looking over my shoulder. Afraid to go to sleep without hearing the clank of metal doors.

Simple things were emotional. Walking into a store and choosing my own deodorant. Eating fresh fruit. Sleeping in a bed with no bars around it. These were things people took for granted—but not me. Every moment was sacred.

Around that time, something happened that I never saw coming. One day while scrolling through social media, I saw her. Jessica. The love of my life. The girl I had known before everything went wrong. It was like time stopped. Her smile was exactly how I remembered it. I hesitated to reach out—what would she think? Would she even remember me? But I couldn't let the moment pass.

I messaged her. A few hours later, she replied. That reply turned into a conversation, and that conversation turned into late-night phone calls, laughter, and vulnerability. She told me how proud she was of my growth. I told her about the fire I still had in me to live right, to love right. We started to build something real—brick by brick, moment by moment.

Jessica had gone through her own struggles. She had children of her own now. But she welcomed me back into her life with grace, strength, and patience. I knew being with her wasn't just about rekindling a love—it meant stepping into a new role. A partner. A protector. A father figure.

We took our time, but our connection deepened quickly. We had both been through so much—years that shaped us in different ways. She had survived abusive relationships and was reclaiming her own voice and power. I was fresh out of prison, learning how to rebuild from the ground up. We weren't just falling back in love; we were learning who we had each become. There were late-night talks filled with honesty and tears, uncovering wounds and rebuilding trust. I felt a deep responsibility—not just to love her, but to be a place of safety and stability for her and her kids. It was pressure, yes, but it was also purpose. I wanted to be the man she could lean on, the one who would never break her spirit but help heal it. Eventually, we made a bold decision: we eloped across the country. No big ceremony. Just us, God, and the road ahead. That trip changed everything. It wasn't about where we got married—it was about who we were becoming together.

But even as our love grew, life was not without its challenges. Around that time, Jessica was going through it with her oldest son. He was struggling, caught in the grip of the streets and spiraling into trouble. I tried to reach him. I poured into him the best I could, hoping my voice would connect. But unfortunately, he ended up incarcerated. Even more painfully, he was forced to accept a plea deal that would impact his entire life, despite having no prior charges. Another example of how the system traps our youth—offering them impossible choices with lifelong consequences. It was heartbreaking watching another young man be swallowed up by the system. Watching another mother cry over her baby. I did my best to support her through it, and to support him as well. I wish I had been there sooner—before the streets and the judicial system got a hold of him. Every time we speak on the phone now, I can hear his soul. And thankfully, because of what I've been through, my voice holds weight. When I tell him, "You can make it, son," I know he believes me.

I became a husband. Jessica's children became a part of my heart too, and I stepped into the role of a father figure in their lives—learning how to lead with love and patience while also continuing to grow as a father to my own children.

Although I stayed connected to God throughout my time inside, I hadn't been to church or attended any services since my release. I prayed, yes—but my spiritual walk had gone quiet. Jessica changed that. She didn't push me, but she ministered to me through how she lived—through her words, her strength, her faith. She reminded me what it meant to walk with God intentionally, not just in survival mode. She helped me get spiritually centered again. With her by my side, I started to see faith not just as a source of comfort, but as a compass guiding every step.

There were days when I felt like I was still learning how to breathe. Trying to balance freedom, family, and faith felt like walking a tightrope. Some mornings I'd wake up in a cold sweat, not from nightmares— but from the weight of responsibility. I wanted to do everything right. I wanted to be strong for Jessica, dependable for her children, present for my own. But there were moments I questioned if I was enough.

I had to remind myself constantly that healing isn't linear. That even though I was free, I was still healing. I still had prison habits to break. Still had old survival instincts to unlearn. Jessica saw those things. She didn't judge me—she supported me. And that made all the difference.

We were both learning to love from a place of survival. But little by little, we learned to love from a place of peace. It wasn't easy. But it was real. And it was worth it.

Freedom wasn't just about walking out—it was about walking forward. Each day brought new challenges, but I met them head-on. I kept showing up, because I knew my life depended on it. I wasn't just surviving anymore. I was living.

Reflection Questions – Chapter 7: *First Steps to Freedom*

31.   What emotions would you expect to feel after leaving a long, confined situation?

32.   How do you handle overwhelming transitions or big changes?

33.   In what ways can reconnecting with family and community aid in healing?

34.   Why is taking immediate action important after a life-changing event?

35.   How can education and purpose help redefine your identity?

CHAPTER 8: A FATHER AND A FOUNDER

Stepping into freedom was one thing. Learning how to walk in it every day was another.

Jessica and I were both coming out of failed marriages when we reconnected. We were in the middle of finalizing divorces, each carrying wounds but also a desire for peace. Rebuilding love while raising kids wasn't easy, but it taught us patience, respect, and resilience. Life took on a new rhythm— family dinners, school events, bedtime stories, and morning routines. I wasn't just building a new life for myself. I was now part of a blended family, with kids looking to me for strength, stability, and leadership. And every time I looked into their eyes, I knew I couldn't fail.

My son, Maxwell, one of the greatest blessings of my life, came from a previous marriage. He was already a part of my life long before I reconnected with

Jessica. Max and Jessica's youngest child were the same age, which made our blended family even more unique. Every time I looked at Max, I was reminded why I had fought so hard to change. He gave my purpose roots. He was the reason I chose to live different.

It didn't stop there. Through a DNA test, I learned I had a daughter I hadn't known about. That moment was heavy—a rush of guilt, joy, fear, and redemption all at once. I reached out, step by step, trying to build a bond based on truth, love, and patience. It wasn't easy, but it was real. I wanted her to know she wasn't forgotten. That she was loved.

Becoming a father again changed everything. It gave my mission teeth. I wasn't just trying to stay free anymore. I was building something for my children. A legacy.

Out of that legacy came a vision: Max Tough Fitness. It wasn't just a gym. It was a calling. I wanted to create a space where young people—especially those like me, who had been counted out—could come to find their strength again. A place where they could train their bodies, rebuild their minds, and leave better than they came.

Starting the business wasn't easy. I had to hustle, save, research, and pray. I faced rejection, doubt, and obstacles at every turn. But I kept showing up. I kept putting in the work. I believed that if I could survive what I had been through, I could build something strong enough to help others survive too.

Max Tough Fitness grew from an idea into a movement. We started hosting fitness boot camps, mentoring sessions, and weekend workshops. Kids came in quiet and broken and left sweating and smiling. I saw pieces of myself in all of them.

Some of the most powerful moments came after the workouts. That's when the real work started. I'd sit with a young man and hear his story. I'd see the anger behind his silence. The pain behind his eyes. And I'd share mine. Not to impress, but to connect. To say, "I see you. I've been there. But you don't have to stay there."

Fatherhood gave me vision. Mentorship gave me drive. Faith gave me foundation. I was no longer defined by my past. I was now a builder of futures.

Reflection Questions – Chapter 8: *A Father and a Founder*

36.   How has becoming a parent or mentor shaped your sense of purpose?

37.   What legacy do you want to leave behind for your children or community?

38.   How can your story help someone else find strength?

39.   In what ways has your pain shaped your passion?

40.   What vision are you building that goes beyond yourself?

CHAPTER 9: FORGIVENESS IS FREEDOM

For a long time, I thought forgiveness was about other people. I thought it meant letting people off the hook who didn't deserve it. People who never apologized. People who took without giving back.

But as I matured, I learned that forgiveness is a gift you give yourself.

I held on to a lot of pain. Pain from the justice system that snatched my youth. Pain from betrayal, abandonment, and being misunderstood. Pain from the lies that led to my incarceration. For years, I carried it all like a chain around my spirit.

I used to fantasize about revenge. About proving everyone wrong. About making people feel the way I felt. But that never gave me peace. It only fueled the anger that held me captive even after I was free.

Then one day I realized—holding onto all of that didn't make me strong. It made me stuck. Stuck in a version of myself I didn't want to be anymore.

The hardest person to forgive was me. I had to face the choices I made, the people I hurt, and the opportunities I threw away. I had to stop running from my reflection and learn to sit with it. And when I did, something powerful happened. I saw the growth. The fight. The heart. I saw a man who didn't give up.

And when I finally forgave myself, it became easier to forgive others.

I forgave the man who lied on me. I forgave the prosecutor who twisted the truth. I forgave the guards who dehumanized me. I forgave the people who didn't come to visit. I forgave the ones who said I'd never make it.

Forgiveness didn't make what happened okay. It just made me free.

Free to be a better father. Free to love without fear. Free to move forward.

That freedom showed up in my relationships too. I stopped looking at everyone like they were out to hurt me. I stopped waiting for betrayal and started expecting love. Jessica saw that change in me. She noticed how my tone shifted, how I started to pray more openly, how I laughed more with the kids. Forgiveness made room for joy. Real joy.

I even reached out to people I never thought I would speak to again. One day, I decided I wanted to confront the person who lied on me—not to lash out, but to let him know how his words had changed the course of my life. I wanted to look him in the eye and explain what his lie had cost me—my freedom, my youth, my peace. But when I looked him up, I found out he had passed away.

That news hit me in a strange way. I remembered that night—how the police had threatened him, told him that if he didn't follow through with the charges, they would press charges on him. It didn't make what he did right, but it reminded me how the system manipulates people too. He wasn't just a liar; he was scared. Caught in something bigger than both of us.

Some people I reached out to responded with regret. Others didn't respond at all. But it didn't matter. The healing wasn't in their reaction. It was in my release.

Now, when I speak to young men who are holding on to anger, I look them in the eye and say, "You've already done the time. Don't do it twice in your mind. Forgive—so you can really live."

Because I know what it's like to be free on paper but imprisoned in your soul. And I know what it feels like to finally, truly let go.

Forgiveness gave me my life back.

Reflection Questions – Chapter 9:
Forgiveness Is Freedom

41.   Who are you still holding anger toward, and why?

42.   What would it feel like to finally let that burden go?

43.   How has unforgiveness affected your mental and emotional health?

44.   What steps can you take toward forgiving yourself?

45.   How might forgiveness free you to pursue your purpose more fully?

CHAPTER 10: PURPOSE THROUGH THE PAIN

By the time I fully embraced forgiveness, something inside me shifted. I was no longer surviving. I was living. And not just living—but walking in purpose.

The idea for Max Tough Fitness didn't just come from my love of working out. It came from a fire to build something that would outlast me. I knew I couldn't undo the past, but I could shape the future—for my kids, for my community, for the youth still teetering on the edge.

I started small. A few borrowed weights. A corner in a park. A flyer here and there. But behind every rep and every session was intention. I wasn't just training bodies—I was reaching souls.

Some of the youth who came through were just like me: angry, misunderstood, disconnected. Others just needed someone to believe in them. I became that someone. Not because I had all the answers, but because I knew their questions. I had lived them.

Max Tough Fitness became more than a gym. It became a movement. A safe haven. A second chance.

But even purpose has growing pains. Balancing business, marriage, fatherhood, and healing wasn't easy. There were days I questioned if I was doing enough. Nights I laid awake wondering if I was really built for this. But every doubt was met with a reminder: I had already survived the worst. Now, I was building something better.

Speaking engagements followed. Schools. Youth centers. Churches. I shared my story with young people who looked at me with wide eyes and nodding heads. Some had already caught charges. Some were on the brink. Some had lost hope.

One young man came up to me after a talk and said, "I'm where you were. I thought I was alone." I hugged him and told him, "You're not. Not anymore."

Every word I spoke, every hand I shook, was part of my redemption. I was no longer just telling my story— I was using it to rewrite others'.

This purpose wasn't pain-free. But it was powerful. And it was worth it.

Reflection Questions – Chapter 10: *Purpose Through the Pain*

46. What is something painful from your past that might contain purpose?

47. How can sharing your story help someone else find healing?

48. In what ways can purpose and pain coexist?

49. What legacy are you building right now, even in your struggles?

50. Who can you reach today that you once couldn't?

CHAPTER 11: REDEMPTION IN MOTION

This journey started in darkness—in confusion, betrayal, and pain. I was just a kid when the system swallowed me whole, when my dreams were shattered, and my faith tested. But somehow, through it all, I survived.

More than that, I was reborn. I made a decision that changed everything: I accepted Jesus Christ into my life. For years I had felt God's presence—especially in the darkest places—but this time, I surrendered fully. I didn't just believe; I committed. And not long after, I was water baptized. What made that moment even more special was that I wasn't alone. Jessica, her children, and even Max all chose to be baptized with me. We stood together as a family—one body, one faith, one step closer to God. Watching each of them go under and rise up again felt like we were washing away generations of pain, starting fresh as a united, faith-led family.

That moment was one of the most powerful of my life. As I stood in the water, I felt the weight of my past rising to the surface. The doubt, the shame, the guilt—all of it. And when I came up, I felt clean. Free. New. It wasn't just symbolic—it was sacred. A line in the sand between who I was and who I had become.

I don't wear my past like a chain anymore. I wear it like armor. Not to protect me, but to remind me what I've been through—and what I've overcome. Every scar has a story, and every story has a purpose.

I used to think redemption was something you had to earn, but I've come to understand it's something you walk in. Step by step. Day by day. With intention, humility, and courage.

My life now is not perfect. I still wrestle with thoughts. Still face temptation. Still have moments where doubt creeps in. But the difference is—I know who I am now. I know whose I am.

I'm a father, a husband, a mentor, a business owner. A man of faith. A voice for the voiceless. And most of all, I'm a survivor of the belly of the beast.

The gym may no longer be open, but the mission continues. I still travel to speak with kids in schools, detention centers, and churches—wherever the message is needed. I also work as a personal trainer, pouring into clients both physically and mentally, using every session as a way to inspire transformation from the inside out.

This book, this mission, this movement—it's all proof that God can use broken pieces to build something unbreakable.

If you're reading this and you've ever felt forgotten, trapped, or unworthy—know this: your story isn't over. You are more than your worst mistake. You are not beyond redemption.

Keep walking. Keep believing. Keep building.

Because the same God who brought me through, will do the same for you.

I made it out the belly of the beast. By the grace of God, I'm still moving forward. And now—it's your turn.

The Belly Of The Beast

Reflection Questions – Chapter 11: *Redemption in Motion*

51.   What does redemption mean to you right now?

52.   What scars do you carry that might hold purpose?

53.   Who are you becoming through your pain and perseverance?

54.   How can your journey be a light for someone else?

55.   What steps can you take today to keep your motion toward healing and purpose?

ACKNOWLEDGMENTS

First and foremost, I want to thank God—for mercy, for grace, for pulling me out of darkness and giving me a second chance. None of this would be possible without You.

To my mother, thank you for your strength, your sacrifices, and your prayers. You never gave up on me, even when I gave up on myself.

To Jessica—thank you for your love, patience, and resilience. You've walked with me through the fire and helped me find peace. I love you more than words can say.

To my children, you are my reason and my fuel. Every step I take is for you.

To the rest of my family—thank you for supporting me, praying for me, and believing in who I could become.

To those who mentored me, wrote me, visited me, or encouraged me when I was locked up—your words helped keep my spirit alive.

To my community, especially the youth I've worked with and the people of Camden—this story is for you. May it be a reminder that your past does not define your future.

And to anyone who ever doubted me—thank you too. You helped build the fire that drives me every day.

Much love and respect,

— Kenneth Scott

AUTHOR'S NOTE

This book isn't just a story—it's my truth. Every chapter, every scar, every prayer and every piece of pain you'll read is real. I didn't write this to be famous. I wrote it so the next person who feels forgotten, broken, or boxed in by the system knows they're not alone.

I was just a teenager when my life was taken off course. The streets raised me, the system tried to erase me, and for a while, I didn't know if I'd ever find my way back. But God had other plans.

Through it all—prison, betrayal, heartbreak, growth, redemption—I found something bigger than survival. I found purpose.

If you're reading this and you've been through hell, if you've sat behind bars or felt trapped in your own mind, know this: there's still a way out. Not just from the outside—but from within.

This book is for the misunderstood, the misjudged, the underestimated. It's for the ones who know what it's like to fight silent battles and keep walking anyway.

Thank you for picking up my story. I pray it inspires you to keep moving, keep believing, and never stop reaching for the light—even in the darkest places.

— Kenny Scott

The Belly Of The Beast

Made in the USA
Columbia, SC
29 August 2025

61647486R00050